Corals and Fishes around Koh Tao in the Gulf of Thailand

A marine biology guide for use during a beginners dive course

Dr. Marc Luxen

ISBN: 9781980712244
Cover: Nick Hobgood

Information and questions: info@duikeninthailand.com

Preface

If you want to get most out of your diving from the first dive, this is THE book for you. Many people go to Asia to learn how to dive, and most of them go to Koh Tao. This book is focused on marine life around Koh Tao, but it is certainly good to use when diving on a tropical coral reef anywhere in the world. The weird thing about seeing things in nature is that you have to know what to see. If it has no name, and you do not know where to look, you probably will not see it.

Especially as a novice diver you need all the help you can get to understand the underwater world around you. Instructors try their best of course, but they cannot tell you everything and at the same time teach you how to dive. If you read this book before you go diving, you will know, I think, everything you need to know to make the most of your diving course.

I am not a biologist, but I do understand the life under water, diving, and writing. Firstly, because I studied evolutionary psychology, and thus knew a thing or two about biology. Secondly, because I have made thousands of dives around Koh Tao, and know what lives there and how it lives. Thirdly, because I have already written a few books on diving subjects, and I am not afraid to look up things that I do not know and to write them down in clear language. I hope, but I also really think that this book will make your dive course much more interesting and fun.

Contents

Corals and Fishes around Koh Tao in the Gulf of Thailand 1
   Preface 3
   Introduction 7
   Natural selection and Sexual Selection 7
   Ecosytems 9
   Plankton 10
   Living together on the coral reef 11
   Colours on the reef 11
   Life underwater 12
   Sponges 12
   Cnideria 13
   Sea anemones 13
   Jellyfish 14
   Coral 14
   Christmas tree worm 16
   Echinoderms Sea cucumbers, starfish and sea urchins: 17
      Sea cucumbers 17
      Starfish 18
      Sea urchins 18
   Nudibranchs 19
   Sea turtles 19
      Green Turtle 20
      The Hawksbill turtle 20
   Cartilaginous Fish 21
      Bluespotted ribbontail ray. 21
      Whale shark 21
      Black tip reef shark 22
   Bony Fish 22
      Barracudas 22
      Yellowtail Barracuda 22
      Chevron Barracuda 23
      Giant Barracuda 23
      Trevally 23
      Yellowspotted Travelly 23
      Giant Trevally 23
      Groupers 24
      Blacktip grouper 24
      Bluespotted grouper 24
      Honeycomb grouper 24
      Clownfish 25
      Pink Anemonefish 25

Harlequin Grouper	26
Red Breasted Wrasse	26
Moon Wrasse	27
Bluestreak Cleaner Wrasse	27
Butterflyfish	27
Moray eel	28
Rabbitfish	28
Bannerfish	28
Titan Triggerfish	29
Angelfish	29
Damsel fish	30
Parrotfish	30
Batfish	30
Pufferfish	31
Goby (with Pistol Shrimp)	31
Yellow-lipped Sea Krait	31
Illustraties	33
Index	35

Introduction

While you are diving, even in your first course, you are curious about what is happening around you under water. This is a very short introduction to marine biology that you can use during your beginners dive course. It is about life in the Gulf of Thailand, and especially Koh Tao, but of course the general principles apply everywhere. My guiding principle in choosing what to include here was: what are you most likely to see as a novice diver?

In the general section at the beginning you will read about Natural Selection and Sexual Selection, Ecosystems, Plankton, living together on the reef and the theory behind animal colours. Then you will read about specific animals that you will see a lot during your dives: Coral, Jellyfish and Anemones, Sea cucumbers, Sea stars and Sea urchins, Nudibranchs, Turtles, Sharks and many colourful fish

You will see the names of all animals in English, and also the scientific Latin name. The Latin name is important because it is the only way to know exactly what species we are talking about, because often species have many local names. The Latin name of animals always consists of two names: Genus and Species, so for us humans that would be: our genus is *Homo* and our species is *sapiens*. I will also tell you what the name means and where it comes from. *Homo* is man in Latin, and *sapiens* means thinking.

But let us start with some general information about life on earth.

Natural selection and Sexual Selection

Figure 1 Everest

The earth is 4.5 billion years old, but most of that time there were only viruses and bacteria. But then, all of a sudden, 600 million years ago, all kinds of life appear in their original form in the ocean. Now, of course, the number of 600 million years does not mean anything to you, so let's find a way to really understand how long that is. Imagine the huge Mount Everest in the Himalayas. This highest mountain in the world is almost nine kilometres (5.6 miles) high. If you could walk up in an ordinary pace, you would have to do more than two hours. Now, mountains are slowly eroding, about a tenth of a millimetre (0.004 inch) a year, say the thickness of a hair. This very high mountain loses a hair of stone per year. How long does it take before the whole mountain is gone? By no means 600 million years! It only takes about 90 million years to turn Everest into a beach. In 600 million years you can do this more than 6 times. That is how long 600 million years are, and that is how long ago life evolved in the sea. Some species have been swimming in exactly the same form for the last 200 million years, such as turtles and sharks. That is incredible; you can build up the Himalayas, demolish them and rebuild them at that time!

A niche in nature is a sort of the gap in the market. It is the specific way in which a species can make a living: cleaning big fish, chipping coral with sharp teeth, sifting the sand for edible waste, these all are niches. That is why evolution has produced so many different species. There are a lot of gaps in the market, niches.

Species split, get extinct, or continue to exist, they split again, and so on and on, already for 600 million years. As soon as a mistake is made in copying a gene, and this error results in that life form being slightly better adapted than the old life form OR that the new life form uses a new niche (way of life, of the environment), a new species starts to evolve. Whether mistakes becomes a species or not depends on selection: the new life form succeeds in surviving and reproducing, or not. This is called **natural selection.**

There are different ways how species can reproduce, and under water you can see about all possibilities. There is **asexual reproduction:** simply dividing yourself into pieces; this is called **parthogenesis** (from the Greek *parthenos*, virgin and *gignesthai*, creating, where for example also "generator" comes from.) But as you know very well there is also **sexual reproduction** through sperm and egg cells. Many forms of life do both in the course of their life span: sometimes they reproduce sexually and sometimes asexually, and there is a very interesting reason for this. Of course it is much easier and cheaper (in terms of energy and effort) just to split yourself to make two of you, but there is a the disadvantage for life forms that are stuck like plants and coral: you cannot really spread out quickly. Another disadvantage of asexual reproduction is that everyone has exactly the same genes, Genetic variation is necessary to resist a virus or bacterium that cracks the genetic code, and if everyone has the same code, like it is the case with asexual reproduction, it can wipe out a whole population at one lucky mutation. The solution to both problems, spreading and genetic diversity, is **sexual reproduction**, where you can mix genes, and you can make from a sperm cell and an egg cell an intermediate form of life that can move., like a larva.. Or, to put it another way: asexual reproduction is using a lucky stroke of finding a resource in the environment and to use it as quickly as you can, it is having a winning ticket, and sexual reproduction is to buy lots of different tickets and see if you can win the main prize.

Once there is sexual reproduction, either everyone produces sperm and egg cells, or just one of the two. Forms that produce both eggs and sperm are **hermaphrodite** (from the Greek gods Hermes - messenger and Aphrodite lust), and this is in fact most common in nature. You can also have men and women and women of course. Incidentally, these forms do not have to remain the same throughout life: many species of fish, such as the Clownfish for example (Nemo), can change sex: these are **sequential hermaphrodites**: from male to female is called **protandreus** = first man, from the Greek *proto* first and *androi*, man), from woman to man is

Figure 2 Peacock's tail

protogyn = first woman, from the Greek *gyne*, woman,

When you have two sexes you have **sexual selection**: the two sexes will choose each other. Usually one is pickier than the other, and that is the sex that invests the most in the posterity: the egg cell carrier, the female form. The best known example of sexual selection is the tail of the male peacock. Such a tail does not really help with survival, so it cannot have been the result of natural selection. In fact, it makes survival more difficult, and this is the reason why women want that tail: if you can keep such a tail as man, you have good genes, and grew up in good environment. Sexual competition usually comes down to women who choose, and men who compete with each other.

So you see that natural selection and sexual selection can counteract each other: natural selection makes inconspicuous and efficient properties, and sexual selection striking and inefficient properties. The banner of a Banner Fish, the colours on of fish, and much more examples abound in nature (ever wondered why the penis in humans has no bone?).

The most bizarre combinations occur in the sea. For example, in the deep open water of the ocean it is difficult for women and men to find each other. If that happens by chance, it is better not to let go of each other. In some fish this happens literally: the male attaches itself to the body of the woman (men are smaller in many species than women, because sperm cells can be much smaller than egg cells), and is then completely digested by the woman, until he is only a pouch of sperm. Bizarre in our eyes, but evolutionary a very good solution.

Ecosytems

Nothing on earth lives isolated. All life forms are connected: they share a part of the world, they eat each other, fight each other, spread each other's seed and eggs, and live from each other's dead material, to name just a few ways how they can be connected. We call this whole system an

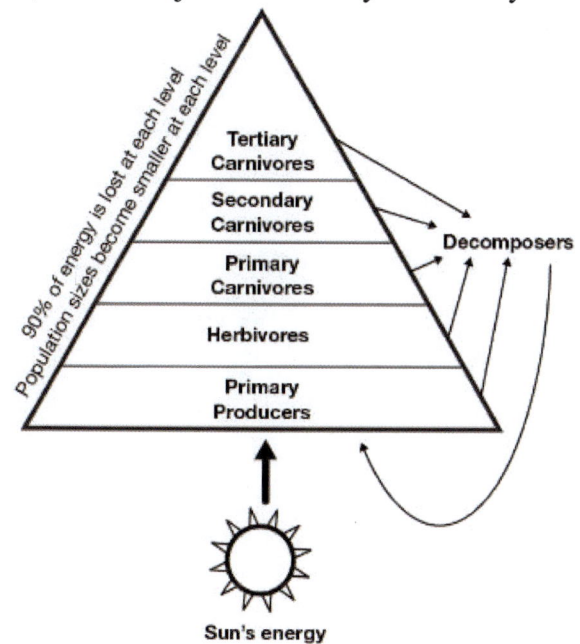

Figure 3 Ecosystem as a pyramid

ecosystem. The ocean is a large ecosystem, and within the ocean we have smaller ecosystems. A coral reef is one of those ecosystems.

The easiest way to imagine an ecosystem is like a pyramid where energy goes from bottom to top. The bottom layer consists of life forms that use energy from the sun to grow. On the land these are plants, in the sea these are seaweeds, sea grass and algae. They are called the **primary producers**. They are the only life forms that actually produce anything. The rest of the animals in the ecosystem simply eat each other. The first step above the producers are the life forms that eat plants and algae: the **herbivores** (from Latin *herba*, plant, and *vorare*, to devour). They are also called **primary consumers**. On land there are animals that eat plants, such as cows, mice and birds (but of course no birds of prey). Under water these are shells, sponges Parrotfish, Rabbitfish Damselfish and Butterflyfish for instance. Damselfish even tend their own garden where they grow algae and they defend when you get close. Usually these fish are not that good to eat because they taste like algae.

The second layer in the pyramid are the first meat-eaters, the **primary carnivores** (from Latin *caro*, meat and *vorare*, to devour). They eat the herbivores. On land, for example, cats, dogs, and birds of prey. Underwater, it is mainly squid, and small predatory fish. They in turn are eaten by, you guessed it, the second meat eaters (**secondary carnivores**), and all higher layers of carnivores of predator fish. Carnivores eat carnivores, and they are eaten by even higher carnivores. How many steps there are depends on the ecosystem and on the person who describes it, but more than five steps actually never occurs.

There is one last group of organisms in the ecosystem: the **decomposers**, which eventually clears the excrement and dead bodies. These are fungi and bacteria. They break everything down into basic building blocks, that the primary producers can then use again. And so the ecosystem lives on until some disaster happens or we people come over, which usually comes down to the same thing.

This transmission of energy is called the **food chain**, but it is actually not a chain, because energy moves horizontally within layers. It is more a **food network**. The thing is that with every step up in the pyramid, ninety per cent of the energy is lost! This means that you need a lot of living creatures to maintain a carnivore at the highest level. So an ecosystem can have many more primary carnivores than higher carnivores, and more of those carnivores than even higher carnivores, until you reach the top. On land these are lions, for example, and under water for example sharks and tuna. To produce a tuna, an ecosystem requires a great deal of time and energy. They are expensive, and if you remove too many of them, the entire ecosystem collapses. That is why eating fish responsibly is "eating low on the food chain". You will know the problem on the land as eating meat: it costs ten times more energy to make a kilo of meat than to produce plants with the same nutritional value.

For us divers, there is an important task here. If we are willing to pay money to go diving and look at the fish instead of eating them, it is in everyone's interest, including the local population, to protect ecosystems. They can earn money from it without destroying it.

Plankton

Plankton, *plankton* means floating, roaming thing in Greek, and they are microscopic algae, plants and animals that float and swim around in the sea. They are at the base of the food chain, and many fish (including most whales) live on it. Sometimes you see the term **nekton** next to plankton: Plankton cannot swim, but nekton can. Many biologists no longer use the term nekton; I will not do that either. Specific types of plankton gets the name of the group they belong to or from: **phyto-plankton** (from plants, *phyton* is a plant in Greek), **zoöplankton** (from animals, *zoö* is animal in Greek), **mycoplankton** (from fungi, *mykes* is mushroom in Greek) and **bacterioplankton** (you already understood that one). By far most plankton floats in temperate seas and polar seas. There you will also find most plankton eaters such as whales and large schools of fish such as herring. Fun fact: fish has so many **omega-3 fatty acids** because they get it from the plankton and the algae they eat (or from eating fish that eat it, etc.). Tropical seas are often poor in nutrients such as nitrate and phosphate, and they are called ocean deserts.

Living together on the coral reef

So far we have only talked about predator-prey relationships, who-eats-who, but that is not the only way organisms live with each other. Some species benefit from other species without eating each other. They have found a niche in each other. We call this kind of relationships **symbiotic relationships** (the word comes from the Greek '*sym*', with, and '*bios*' life) There are three types of symbiotic relationships:

Figure 4 Symbiosis: commensalism between shark and remora

1) **Mutualism** (from the Latin *mutuus*, which means mutually) in which both organisms profit from each other. Examples of mutualism are flowers and bees: the flowers get their pollen spread out, and the bees get food. Underwater there are cleaning fish that clean other fish from parasites by eating them and by doing this it keeps the other, the host, healthy.

2) **Commensalism** (from Latin *com*, with and *mensa*, table), where only one organism benefits from the relationship, but it does not harm the other organism. Examples of commensalism are vultures that follow predators to eat the remains of their prey, and underwater sharks followed by smaller fish that use their wake: the predators and the sharks do not benefit from it, but they do not suffer any damage either.

3) **Parasitism** (from the Greek *para*, alongside, and *sitos*, food), where one organism benefits from the relationship, and thus is harmful to the other organism. Our parasites are for example tapeworms (and children). There are also fish that imitate a cleaner fish and take a bite out of the host instead of removing parasites from the skin.

Colours on the reef

The most logical colour to have as an animal is a colour that does not stand out, especially when you are a prey animal. You have a protective colour and you are camouflaged. **Camouflage** is therefore the first reason why animals have the colours they have. Camouflage is a result of natural selection: if you do not notice you are more likely to survive.

The second way how colour is determined goes directly against this, and is the result of sexual selection (think of the Peacock's tail). Sexual selection is different for men and women, and so, unlike camouflage, it usually results in differences between men and women. It is usually the males who stand out and show that they do not need camouflage at all, and so they are coloured. You can of course also use colour temporarily, only during the breeding season. Above the water you know this from a lot of birds, underwater many fish with colours do exactly the same.

The third way how an animal's colour is determined is warning colours. They are striking because they warn: "you do not want me. I can hurt you, or I'm poisonous if you eat me". This is therefore a consequence of natural selection. You know this from wasps, for example, and under water his sea snakes are a good example.

Figure 5: A fake eye on a Butterflyfish

The fourth way is fascinating way evolution works: you can of course take over the warning colours of another, for instance a really dangerous species, and pretend you are dangerous while you are not. This is called **mimicry**, and you know that above water from flies that imitate wasps (some biologists claim that cats imitate snakes ...). Underwater the most striking mimicry is the false cleaner wrasse: it mimics the real cleaner wrasse, but doesn't clean a fish but takes a bite out of it. Mimicry is also the result of natural selection.

Lastly, there is a striking pattern: a **fake eye**. Some fish have a black dot on their back that looks like a big eye. This protects them from attacks: they look bigger and if they are attacked it is at the back (you probably know this from butterflies). So this is a special case of mimicry. If you think of a Peacock's tail now, then you see that the whole tail comes through sexual selection, and the eyes to get the costs in terms of being eaten down by means of mimicry. This is therefore sexual selection and natural selection together. You can also see this everywhere under water.

Life underwater

Roughly speaking, we see two large groups while diving in the tropics. Animals without a backbone, **invertebrates,** and animals with a backbone like us, **vertebrates**. Invertebrates are much older, and stranger: coral, anemones, sea cucumbers, shells and jellyfish for example. Vertebrates are all fish and mammals such as dolphins and whales. Let's start with the invertebrates, because you are guaranteed to see a lot of them.

Figure 6 Red Tube Sponge

Sponges

Sponges (*Porifera* = hole carriers) are primitive: some can even be pushed through a sieve so that all cells are separated, and those cells find each other again in a few hours and make new sponges. We still see them everywhere underwater, more or less in the same form, they have been around all those 500,000,000 years. They live by filtering plankton out of the water, and reproduce by releasing sperm and egg cells. If these find each other, they become a sponge larva in the plankton, which can then find a new place to start.

Cnideria

Cnidaria (Greek *Cnida* is nettle, actually the same word). are **coral**, **anemones** (*Anthozoa* = flower animals) and **jellyfish** (*Scyphozoa* = bowl animals). These animals are therefore closely related. They eat plankton that they pick from the water with their tentacles. Usually the tentacles only come out at night, during the day they are withdrawn. Coral, anemones and jellyfish also have a second way to get food. They have a symbiotic relationship with an alga with the annoying name ***zooxanthellae*** (*zoö* is an animal in Greek, *xanthos* is yellow) that both benefit from (a mutualistic relationship). Zoox, like plants, can make energy from sunlight.

Sea anemones

Figure 7 Sea Anemone

Sea anemones (*Actinia,* from the Greek *Actia,* radius, because they are symmetrical) are named after the flower the Anemone because they are just as colourful. They are not plants, but animals that catch their prey, shells and small fish, with their poisonous tentacles, and bring them to their mouth in the middle of their body. They have only one opening: their mouth is also their anus. They have no central nervous system, but a primitive nervous system that consists of two parts, one on top for perceiving and one at the bottom for moving, that connect at the mouth (or anus). They can slowly crawl over the bottom, and they sometimes hitch a ride on the back of a crab.

Sea anemones breed sexually with egg cells and sperm cells and asexually through parthogenesis (splitting yourself). They release egg cells and sperm cells that become *larvae* in the plankton. These larvae find a spot, and form a polyp; they do not become a medusa first (a **medusa** is small jellyfish, after the Greek monster Medusa, who had her snakes on her head instead of her hair), as all the other *cnideria* do. Some species have men and women, and some species are sequential hermaphrodites and change sex during their lifetime.

Many anemones have a symbiosis with clown fish who live among their poisonous tentacles. The Clownfish is however not immune to the poison, but the anemone simply does not attack the Clownfish. It does have a thick mucus layer as extra protection. There is a lot of confusion as to their exact relation, but anemones with an anemone fish grow faster than anemones without them. I have read that clownfish provide the anemones more oxygen by moving, that they attract fish to the anemone, that they attack fish that want to eat anemone, and that they put pieces of fish that are too big for them directly to the anemone. We simply do not really know, but in any case, it is clear that they live in symbiosis, and that is a mutualistic symbiosis.

Jellyfish

Jellyfish (***Scyphozoans***, Greek *scypho*, bowl, and *zoön*) are meat eaters that eat plankton, shellfish, fish and other jellyfish. They catch their prey with their poisonous tentacles. They can be very small, just a few millimetres, or huge with a hat of more than 2 meters, and a weight of 200 kilos. The tentacles of the longest jellyfish ever measured were more than 35 meters, and who

Figure 8 Jellyfish

knows what else is swimming around in the deep sea. They have no brains, but a simple nervous system in the hat and tentacles.

Jellyfish are the energy efficient swimmers: they use only half of the energy that other animals use:

https://www.youtube.com/watch?v=MmqfrJgakH4

They reproduce in different phases A jellyfish (a *medusa*) splits off from a polyp attached to the bottom. The jellyfish grows, and then releases sperm and egg cells. When these encounter each other, they become a larva that seeks a spot on the bottom, and grows into a small polyp, usually only a few millimetres large. The polyp can continue to exist in this form for years, and splits off jellyfish that…etc. etc.

This means they reproduce asexually and sexually. The jellyfish itself (the medusa) is the way of sexual reproduction: most jellyfish are either male or female. Polyps can then reproduce asexually by splitting. There may even be an immortal jellyfish than can change into a polyp again from the jellyfish form, and thus do not ever die.

To protect yourself from jellyfish stings, even a thin layer of protection like nylon stocking is enough, surprisingly. This is because the stinging cells are not triggered by pressure, but by chemicals on the skin. If they cannot detect these through the nylon, they do not fire. Jellyfish bites should be treated by scraping the area with a razor or credit card (gloves!) to remove all cells, and then rinsing with hot salt water. Fresh water, vinegar, and alcohol, and urine only make it worse, although older texts still recommend it!

Figure 9 Staghorn coral
Albert Kok

Coral

Most open seas are very poor in food. You can see them as deserts. Most animals that you can find there are on their way to somewhere else, somewhere where there is food, to oases in the desert. A **coral reef** is such an oasis. A coral reef offers protection and food for many species of fish, and it is one of the most fascinating ecosystems in the world.

Coral is an animal, just like a jellyfish and an anemone. You can imagine coral as an inverted jellyfish, but one that cannot swim, because it built a calcium tunnel around itself. With millions together they form a colony; a coral reef, on stones and rocks. Layer after layer they live on the lime of old coral polyps, and so they build a reef. A coral polyp itself is only a few years old, but the reefs they build can be ten thousand years old, and even more so. The most beautiful form of a coral reef is an atoll: a ring-shaped reef that started around a volcanic island that sank, while the reef kept growing outwards and upwards, and thus grows around a lake, where the volcano once was.

Coral fights with each other for space, by extending their stomachs and eating each other. You can see that happening here

Figure 10 Brain coral

https://www.youtube.com/watch?v=5UHKFlig9qM

Figure 12 Star coral

Coral reproduces by splitting (asexual) or sexually by releasing sperm and egg cells in the water, which become a larva, just like sponges. These larvae then become a medusa, a mini jellyfish, and this seeks a place to settle. In order to ensure that the sperm and eggs can find each other, coral times spawning by monitoring use temperature changes, the length of the day and the cycle of the moon; they spawn at sunrise.

Coral is a very effective hunter. With their tentacles they can catch up to 95% of all the plankton that flows over them. Some species have a symbiotic relationship with zooxanthallae, an algae that, like a plant, extract energy from sunlight. Corals that live deeper down, where there is almost no sunlight, do not need a zoox, and catch all their food themselves. Without zoox, shallow coral can survive for a while, but cannot grow. When the temperature gets too high, the coral cannot hold onto zoox for some reason, and expels it. With the zoox all colour disappears, and the coral reef becomes stone white: coral bleaching.

Figure 11 Table coral

Christmas tree worm

The **Christmas tree worm** (*Spirobranchus giganteus* Latin *spiro*, spiral, and *branchus*, branch and *gigas*, enormous size) is a tube worm, which include here behind corals because they live in the coral, and you always see them together. It is a worm that digs into the coral as a larva, and then becomes a worm of about 10 centimetres. They build a tube around them, and then let their colourful spiral tentacles reach out, two brightly coloured crowns with which they breathe and catch plankton. I have no idea why they are so colourful and why there are so many colours, but it is probably not sexual selection: they propagate by spawning eggs and sperm cells in the water; they are male or female. Neither are the colours a warning, because they are non-toxic. They can get up to forty years old and have a fairly developed central nervous system. They pull their tentacles at the slightest danger. They have a mutualistic relationship with the coral, which gives them a safe place: as a service they keep the dreaded crown of thorns away by pushing on their bottoms with their crowns.

Figure 13 Coral Bleaching
CC BY 3.0, https://en.wikipedia.org/w/index.php?curid=32829631

Figure 14 Christmas tree worm

Echinoderms Sea cucumbers, starfish and sea urchins:

Sea cucumbers, starfish and sea urchins are ***Echinoderms*** (= from the Greek *echinos*, hedgehog and *derma*, skin). They have been there for about 500 million years, and they only live in salt water. Most are scavengers, detritus cleaners, like worms on land, and they can survive in nutrient-poor deep seas. They have five rows of miniscule little feet that move slowly. They breed sexually through a larval stage; and sometimes also asexually, just like coral. They can even grow back completely from a piece of body. They have no brains, but they do have a reasonably developed nervous system. They have a hydraulic (water pressure-based) system to move around.

Sea cucumbers

Figure 15 Sea cucumber

Figure 16 Sea cucumber feet/tentacles

Sea cucumbers (***Holothuroidea***, Greek and Latin water-polyp) are indeed a kind of large cucumbers, usually around 10 to 30 cm, lying on the seabed. They come in all shapes and sizes. They sometimes have tentacles around their mouth, and they can also use these to get oxygen from the water (when they stand up right). Some species throw their entrails out when they are touched, like a kind of white threads. They have nerve cells in their skin to be able to feel threats, but they have no real developed nervous system. A nice fact is that they can dissolve the connective tissue from their body, and can become almost liquid, so they can seek protection in small corners and holes. They then simply build up their bodies again. They have tentacles in the form of finely branched trees in their anus, and they suck water over them. So they breathe with their anus.

If you go deeper than 5 km, sea cucumbers make up 90% of the total weight of all life there, and they form large herds that scoop the seabed. They can live up to 10 km deep, which is almost impossible, because there is no sunlight and the pressure is enormous. Just like worms, they eat the soil and grind the sand and stone to filter out food. Thus they play a major role in the formation of the seabed. They are between five and ten years old. Sea cucumbers are consumed in Asia; they are quite tasteless, with a bit of fishy aftertaste.

Starfish

Starfish (*Asteroidea,*, from the Greek *aster*, star, and *eidon* image, that's where our word 'idea' comes from: "the shape of a star"). Starfish usually have a round middle and five arms (sometimes more). They eat shells by pulling the two halves a bit apart, and then pushing a part of their intestines into them, so they digest the food inside. This allows them to eat prey that is much larger than their mouth: oysters, shrimps, and even small fish.

They have no brains, but they do have a complicated nervous system, which consists of two parts: an upper part to feel, see, and smell, and lower part to move. Starfishes are therefore

Figure 17 Crown of thorns

controlled by a central nervous system, so they cannot plan anything: if one of the legs detects food, it takes over the control of the whole starfish and thus moves towards the source.

Most sea stars breed sexually and asexually, and most species have male and female forms, but there are also hermaphrodites. There are even sequential hermaphrodites that change from male to female. Some species go even so far as that female starfish can split into male pieces, which then become women once they have grown large enough. Starfish can therefore grow from a piece of starfish, and arms that are ripped off just grow back again. This is called **regeneration** (from the Latin *re*, meaning back or again, and the Greek *gignesthai* that means to be born, means creating). Sea stars get about 10 to 15 years old.

A starfish that is important to us divers is called the **Crown of Thorns** (*Acanthaster planci*). It is a prickly and poisonous starfish. I got stung once and for weeks I had a swollen and black hand. They eat coral, and they can become a plague and devour whole coral reefs. Biologists thought they could become a plague because animals that ate them were killed, but that turned out not to be the case. It is more likely that the nutrients in polluted water allow more algae to grow, which enables the larvae of the crown of thorns to survive easily.

Sea urchins

Sea urchins (*Echinoidea*, from the Greek *echinos*, hedgehog, and *eidon*, image, so hedgehock shapes) we all know. They eat algae, shells, small animals and also sea cucumbers, they scrape over rocks and sand with an organ that has the great name **Aristotle's Lantern** (after the

Figure 18 Sea Urchin

Greek philosopher, who was crazy about sea hedgehogs). Their spines are around three centimetres long and are non-toxic, but they break off very easily in your skin, and are difficult to get out. If they become a plague, they can turn whole areas of the ocean into a desert.

Nudibranchs

Figure 19 A Doride Nudibranch

Nudibranchs (**Nudibranchia**, Latin *nudus*, naked, and Greek *branchia*, gills, bronchitis comes from this as well, so pronunciation is NUdeeBranc, and NOT NUdeebranch) are the darlings of many divers because they come in so many different colours and shapes. In this respect they are the song birds of the sea. There are more than 2,300 different species (NOTE: not all marine slugs are the Nudibranchs).

Figure 20 An Aeolide Nudibranch

They are divided into two types: the **Dorids** and **Aeolides** (these names mean nothing, but are borrowed from names of Greek temple architecture). Dorids have a kind of feather attached to their bodies, and Aeolids have a lot of bulges everywhere on their bodies. They are usually a few centimetres in size. Nudibranchs are mostly meat eaters. They crawl across the seabed in search of food. The colour of nudibranchs can be a camouflage (usually sponges or soft coral mimicry) but some also use warning: nudibranchs can be poisonous, as a compensation for losing their houses that other snails still have. They either make their own poison, they get it from their food, or they steal poisonous tentacles of jellyfish and such, which then get the nice name **kleptocnidae** (from the Greek *kleptein*, to steal, where also our kleptomaniac comes from and *cnida*, nettle)

Nudibranchs are hermaphrodites, and have their female and male openings always on the right. They cannot fertilize themselves, and so they must reproduce sexually by releasing eggs and sperm cells, wrapped in a protective slime layer, which then become larvae in the plankton.

Sea turtles

Sea Turtles, (*Chelonia* Greek *Khelone*, turtle). They have been on the earth for around 200 million years, and can therefore rightly be called living fossils. They are cold-blooded, and thus have about the temperature of the environment. Glands close to their eyes secrete the salt from the sea that they ingest. They have strong sharp or ribbed jaws, but no teeth.

Turtles move by swimming with their front legs, and using their hind legs as a rudder. They only come on land to lay eggs and, as a newly born sea turtle, crawl to the sea. They have to come to the surface to breathe. If they move, they can stay under water for about ten minutes, but if they are sleeping, they can stay under water for up to seven hours.

Sea turtles eat jellyfish, sponges, and if they have hard jaws, also shells. The green sea turtle is vegetarian, and only eats algae. Sea turtle eggs are leathery, not hard, and consist almost entirely of yellow (which does not become hard when you cook it). They always return to lay their eggs to the beach where they were born, because it is certain that the conditions are favourable. That can be more than 1500 kilometres of swimming, so they are excellent navigators. They even have magnetic crystals in their heads that function as a compass! The temperature in which the eggs hatch determines the sex: warmer makes women, colder makes men. This means that eggs on the inside of the heap will become women more often and those on the outside more often become men. Young turtles always take care of themselves, there is no parent care.

They can be about a hundred years old, and it is fascinating that their organs do not age at all. The liver, kidneys of a 100 year old are still the same as those of a 5 year old.

Figure 21 Green Turtle
Brocken Inaglory

Green Turtle

The **Green Turtle** (*Chelonia mydas*; *mydas* is wet in Greek) have "green" in their name because their fat is greenish from the algae and seaweed they eat, because they are strict herbivores when they are adults. They are the soup turtles The youngsters however do eat fish and jellyfish. They can grow to 1.5 meters and weigh around 130 kilos. They are closely related to the hawksbill turtle (see below), but they have a short blunt beak. They cannot retract their head. They are long distance swimmers when they return to their birth beach to lay eggs. That can mean more than 2500 kilometres of swimming.

The Hawksbill turtle

The **Hawksbill Turtle** (*Eretmochelys imbricata*; *eretmon* is paddle, *khelone* is turtle, and Imbracata means roofing) has overlapping horn shields on its back, and a sharp, parrot-like beak. You will find them along rocky coasts and shallow waters around the equator. They are about a metre long, weighing around 80 kilos. The sea turtle is not edible because they eat poisonous cnideria such as anemones and store that poison in their bodies

Figure 22 Hawksbill Turtle
magicOlf

Cartilaginous Fish

Cartilaginous Fish (*Chondrichthyes*, from the Greek *chonor*, cartilage and *ichtus*, fish) have no bones, but only cartilage. They have no ribs, and their skin is made of small teeth instead of scales, which protect them and ensure perfect streamlining. They are sharks, rays and sawfish.

Figure 23 Bluespotted Ribbontail Ray
Jens Petersen

Bluespotted ribbontail ray.

The **Bluespotted Ribbontail Ray** (*Tenioura lymma*, *taenia* means stripe, *oura* tail, and *lymma*, dust) is about 35 cm, with a poisonous tail. During the day they are hidden under rocks, and they hunt at night for shells and fish hidden in the sand. They can find it by observing the electricity that everything that lives generates, right through the sand. Females produce live-born young, around seven at a time. They can sting us, but that is very rare: they will always choose to go away instead of fight.

Whale shark

The **Whale Shark** (*Rhincodon typus* from the Greek *rhyngchos* snout, *odontos* tooth and *typos* mark) is the dream of every diver. It is a slow swimming shark that does not eat fish, but plankton. They are therefore completely harmless. So, like whales, they need a big mouth, and therefore a big body. This can be done underwater, because weight does not matter there. Above water, where there is gravity this does not work, and so there are other solutions. A spider weaves a web, which you can actually see as a very big mouth.

They are sharks, and therefore fish. The whale shark is the largest fish that exists. The largest whale shark was more than 12 meters long, but on average they are around nine meters, and weighs 9,000 kilos. Although it is a fish, the babies are born alive. The mother stores the sperm from only one single encounter in her body and then regularly produces young, who are

Figure 24 Whale Shark
Christian Jensen

around fifty centimetres when they swim away. They are only able to reproduce when they are around thirty years old, and they become up to 100 years old.

Black tip reef shark

Figure 25 Blacktip Reefshark
janderk

De **Blacktip Reefshark** (*Carcharhinus melanopterus karcheros* means sharp and *rhinos* nose, *melas* dark, and *optos* visible) is the most common shark around the equator, and everywhere their dorsal fin with the black point can be seen. They get around 1.5 meters long, and they live on the edge of reefs and on sandy stretches, but they also swim up rivers, hunting for fish and squid. They catch sea snakes and even birds, and even eat each other. They stay in the same place for years, shy and fleeing from divers, but in shallow water they can mistake legs for prey.

Bony Fish

Bony Fish (*Osteichthyes* of *ostuon*, bones and *ichtus*, fish) are actually all other fish that we know. They have a real skeleton of bones, ribs, and a skin with scales.

Barracudas

Figure 26 Yellowtail Barracuda
Jens Petersen

Barracudas (*Sphyraena*, from Greek *sfuri*, hammer, which was also used for pike-like fish) are fast hunters, the hawks of the water. Silvery streamlined fish that can shoot through the water at a speed of 40 km per hour. They catch all kinds of fish. In the Gulf of Thailand we usually see three species.

Yellowtail Barracuda

De **Yellowtail Barracuda** (*Sphyraena flavicauda*, *flavus* is yellow, *cauda* is tail) is the smallest, around 20 cm. They hunt in schools around reefs at night.

Chevron Barracuda

Thee **Chevron barracuda** (*Sphyraena genie,* *genie* is spirit in Latin). About 30 cm long, looks a little like a mackerel.

Giant Barracuda

The **Giant Barracuda** (*Sphyraena barracuda*), the dominant predatory fish of the coral reef, can grow to 1.4 meters, and weigh around 100 kilos.

Trevally

We often see two kinds of **Trevally** (*Carangidae* from Greek *karanx*, runner. They are silver predatory fish that shoot through the water, sometimes just in front of divers. The smaller ones in large groups, the large hunting alone or at most with a few

Yellowspotted Travelly

The **Yellowspotted Travelly** *Carangoides fulvoguttatus* usually in small groups, flashing in front of divers.

Figure 27 Chevron Barracuda

Figure 28 Giant Barracuda
Albert Kok

Giant Trevally

The Giant Travelly, (***caranx ignobili*** *ignobilis* is infamous, notorious). Is usually around 1 meter large, and a solitary hunter.

Figure 30 Yellowspotted Travelly

Figure 29 Giant Travelly
Dr. Dwayne Meadows

Groupers

Figure 31 Blacktip Grouper
Alan Slater

Groupers (*Epinephelinae*, Greek for cloudy, misty) come in all shapes and sizes, the largest can weigh 100 kilos. They eat fish, cuttlefish, crabs and lobsters, which they catch by lying motionless, like a pike. With their snouts and gills they can suck in their prey in from a considerable distance. Young grouper are mostly female, and become male when they grow larger (they are protogyn). When they are 3 kilos again they become female, and are adults. Males can have harems. Groupers often hunt for prey together with Moray eels, who can get into crevices where they themselves do not fit into.

Blacktip grouper

The: **Blacktip Grouper** (*Epinephelus fasciatus*, *fasciatus* is striped, same root as fascism) is about 20 cm large, They eat shells and small fish.

Figure 32 Bluespotted Grouper
Adrian Pingstone

Bluespotted grouper

The **Bluespotted Grouper** (*Cephalopholis argus*, *Cephalos* is head, *Argus* comes from a mythical figure with a hundred staring eyes) grows 10 centimetres. They follow large predators such as moray eels.

Honeycomb grouper

The **Honeycomb Grouper** (*hexa* is six, *gonos* is angle) (*Epinephelus merra*, gets about 25 centimetre large. They live and hunt alone, and they are female until they are 16 cm, when they change into adult males.

Figure 33 Honeycomb Grouper
Bernard DUPONT

Yellowtail Fusilier

The **Yellowtail Fusilier** (*Caesio teres*, of Latin *caesium* blue-gray (such as the metal caesium) and *teres*, round, smooth) is about 20 centimetres. They eat zooplankton.

Figure 34 Yellowtail Fusilier
Nhobgood

Clownfish

The **Clownfish** (*Amphiprion ocellaris*, from Greek *amphi*, round or double sided, and *prion*, saw, and Latin *ocellare*, going back and forth) you probably know from the film Nemo. We have already encountered them at the anemones, with which they have mutualistic symbiosis (only the sea anemones of the species, *Heteractis magnifica*, *Stichodactyla gigantea*, and *Stichodactyla mertensii*, if you want to know). The Clownfish lives in small groups of one female, a dominant male, and increasingly smaller males in an anemone. The female only mates with the biggest male. As soon as the female disappears, the dominant male becomes a female, and the next male in the line becomes the dominant male. They are from the same family as the Damselfish.

Figure 35 Clownfish
Nick Hobgood

Pink Anemonefish

The **Pink Anemonefish** (*Amphiprion perideraion* van *peri*, rondom, en *deraion*, halsketting) of *peri*, around, and *deraion*, necklace) lives the same as the anemone fish, but in another anemone.

Figure 36 Pink Anemonefish
Bernd

Harlequin Grouper

The **Harlequin Grouper** (***Plectorhinchus chaetodonoides***, from Greek *plectos*, woven or flat, and *rhyngchos*, muzzle; *chaetodonoides* are butterfly fish) is about 70 cm. They eat shells and corals at night .Why harlequin? Because the juveniles look like a harlequin: this is mimicry, they mimicry a poisonous worm or Nudibranch.

Figure 37 Harlequin Grouper Adult
Richard Ling

Figure 38 Harlequin Grouper Juvenile
Jens Petersen

Figure 37 Redbreasted Wrasse
Jens Petersen

Figure 381 Moon Wrasse
Leonard Low

Red Breasted Wrasse

The **Redbreasted Wrasse** . (***Cheilinus fasciatus***, Greek *cheilos* means lip means, Latin *fasciatus* is striped) is about 35 cm. Lives solitary on sand and loose stones, where they dig for shellfish. They follow trigger fish that disturb the sand, and they approach divers for the same reason.

Moon Wrasse

The **Moon Wrasse** (*Thalassoma lunare*, from Greek *thalassa*, sea (colored), *soma*, body, and Latin *luna*, moon is about 25 cm. It is a beautiful green-blue fish with moon-shaped tail. They live in groups of a dominant males and a group of females. The dominant male has the brightest colours, and at low tide he changes from more green to more blue, and attacks other male fish to show his dominance. During mating season he gathers all the females around him, and spreads his seed around them.

Bluestreak Cleaner Wrasse

The **Bluestreak Cleaner Wrasse** (***Labroides dimidiatus***, from the Latin *labrus*, lip, *di-midiare*, in two parts) are small fishes of around 10 cm. They clean the skin of other fish (and divers!), and use it as food, and thus have a perfect mutualistic symbiosis with all kinds of fish. They work in cleaning stations, often on brain coral, where fish turn themselves upside down to indicate that they want to be cleaned. They even open their mouths for the cleaning fish go inside without being eaten. They often peck at our earlobes because they mistake them for gills. They are protogyne hermaphrodites. We see them every dive. A cleaner wrasse can service up to 300 customers a day. Injured or sick fish will return a few times a day. There are fish that mimic them, to be able take a quick bite out of the host instead of cleaning them.

Figure 39 Bluestreak Cleaner Wrasse
Divervincent

Butterflyfish

Butterflyfish (***Chaetodontidae*** Greek *chaite*, hair, and *odontos*, teeth) become up to 80 cm. They eat invertebrates and coral polyps, and have a territory. They are active in shallow water during the day. At night they sleep in rock crevices and they look different because they take on protective colours

Figure 40 Butterflyfish
Leonardo Stabile

Moray eel

Moray Eel (*Muraenidae*, from the Greek *Moraina*, eel) are long round eels that live in rock crevices. There are more than 200 species. They live on fish and shellfish that they catch in crevices. They can work together with smaller groupers that follow them on a hunt and do not let the fish escape. They look dangerous because they have their mouth with large teeth open, but that is only to breathe. They are only eaten by big groupers, barracudas and sea snakes.

Figure 41 Moray eel (*Gymnothorax thyrsoideus*)
Bernard Dupont

Rabbitfish

Rabbitfish (*Siginidae,* from Latin *sigan (us),* from Arabic *sijaan*, means rabbit fish) is 15 centimetres long. They have poisonous spines on their backs. They live during the day, sometimes alone, sometimes in schools and eat algae.

Figure 44 Masked Spinefood Rabbitfish *Siganus puellus*

Figure 45 Foxface Rabbitfish *Siganus vulpinus*

Figure 42 Bannerfish
fir0002

Bannerfish

The **Bannerfish** (*Heniochus acuminatus*, The only Heniochus I could find was a Greek playwright, *Acuminatus* is sharply pointed) is 15 centimetres. They eat zooplankton. Juveniles live alone and also live of cleaning other fish.

Titan Triggerfish

The **Titan Triggerfish** (*Balistoides viridescens*, from Greek *ballo*, to throw and Latin *viridescens*, to turn green) becomes 75 cm. They have strong teeth to crack open shells and sea urchins that they find on the sand, among stones and pieces of coral that they grab and turn over. Smaller fish follow them, so that they take part of the feeding. In mating season they defend their territory and attack other fish (and us) by swimming up against them.

Angelfish

The **Angelfish** (***Pomacanthi***, *Poma* is Greek for covered and *akantha* thorn become around 50 cm.) They eat sponges, coral and algae, and roam over a large residential area.

Figure 43 Titan Triggerfish
Jan Derk

Figure 45 Sixstripe Angelfish
Leonard Low

Figure 44 Ringed Angelfish

Damselfish

Damselfish (*Pomacentri*, Greek *poma*, covered, *kentros*, thorn) consist of many species They grow up to 20cm. Some keep a garden in corals that they weed and aggressively defend (the farmer fish).

Parrotfish

Parrotfish (*Scaridae,* from the Greek *skairo*, to jump) are 30 cm. There are about 100 species of parrot fish, two subfamilies, all

Figure 47 Damselfish

of which are quite similar and many of them all live in the same area. They are all subspecies of groupers. They are called parrotfish because their teeth resemble the beak of a parrot. They eat the algae in coral by grinding it, and like this they produce the

Figure 46 Parrotfish
CC BY-SA 3.0,
https://commons.wikimedia.org/w/index.php?curid=29 3543

white coral sand. They make about 30 kilos of sand per year. They are protogyne hermaphrodites, which often change colours in their life stages.

Batfish.

Many fish are called **Batfish** genoemd worden, maar hier gaat het over The ***Platax teira***, Greek *platys* is *flat*, and *teira* I have no idea). They become about 70 cm. They eat algae that parrot fish do not eat.

Figure 48 Batfish
Alain Feulvarch

Pufferfish

The **Pufferfish** (***Tetraodontidae*** from the Greek *tetris*, four, and *odontos*, tooth) can blow itself up with water - you often see the skeletons. They eat sponges and coral. The skin and mucous membranes are lethally toxic - this is the fish of the potentially deadly Fugru sushi.

Figure 49 Pufferfish *Sphoeroides spengleri*
Andrew David

Figure 50 Goby and shrimp *Cryptocentrus cinctus* and *Alpheus bellulus*
Nick Hobgood

Goby (with Pistol Shrimp)

The **Gobies** (*Gobiidae*, from the Greek *Kobios*, a species of small fish) are 10 cm. There are more than 2000 species

Gobies often live in symbiosis with **Pistol Shrimp**: The shrimp, that has poor vision, digs a hole in the bottom and keeps it open, and they both then live in it. The goby is on guard, wobbling its tail against the shrimp's antennae to warn of danger. The shrimp first disappears in the hole, then the goby itself.

The Pistol Shrimp is called like that because they can make a loud noise with their legs with which they catch their prey. The sound is strong enough to kill small fish.

Yellow-lipped Sea Krait

The **Yellow-lipped Sea Krait** (***Laticauda colubrine***, Latin *cauda*, tail, *latis*, flat and *coluber*, snake) is about one meter long. Their black and white pattern is a warning colour. They hunt for moray eels and sometimes small fish, which they paralyze with their powerful poison. They are not real sea snakes, because they spend half their time on land, and they have to build their nests on land. They are not aggressive at all, but the old wives' tale that their teeth are too small to bite us is not true (of course not, how else could they hunt?). Very few cases are known when they have bitten people, and there are no deadly cases.

Figure 51 Yellow-lipped Sea Krait

They are in turn eaten by sharks, birds, and big fish, but they defend themselves with mimicry of their own: their tails look like their heads and makes the same movements, and this comes in handy when they are vulnerable exploring a crevice.

Illustraties

Figure 1 Everest..7
Figure 2 Peacock's tail..8
Figure 3 Ecosystem as a pyramid...9
Figure 4 Symbiosis: commensalism between shark and remora..11
Figure 5: A fake eye on a Butterflyfish..12
Figure 6 Red Tube Sponge...12
Figure 7 Sea Anemone..13
Figure 8 Jellyfish..14
Figure 9 Staghorn coral Albert Kok...14
Figure 10 Brain coral..15
Figure 11 Table coral..15
Figure 12 Star coral..15
Figure 13 Coral Bleaching CC BY 3.0, https://en.wikipedia.org/w/index.php?curid=32829631 ...16
Figure 14 Christmas tree worm..16
Figure 15 Sea cucumber...17
Figure 16 Sea cucumber feet/tentacles...17
Figure 17 Crown of thorns...18
Figure 18 Sea Urchin..18
Figure 19 A Doride Nudibranch...19
Figure 20 An Aeolide Nudibranch...19
Figure 21 Green Turtle Brocken Inaglory..20
Figure 22 Hawksbill Turtle magicOlf..20
Figure 23 Bluespotted Ribbontail Ray Jens Petersen...21
Figure 24 Whale Shark Christian Jensen...21
Figure 25 Blacktip Reefshark janderk..22
Figure 26 Yellowtail Barracuda Jens Petersen...22
Figure 27 Chevron Barracuda..23
Figure 28 Giant Barracuda Albert Kok..23
Figure 29 Giant Travelly Dr. Dwayne Meadows...23
Figure 30 Yellowspotted Travelly..23
Figure 31 Blacktip Grouper Alan Slater..24
Figure 32 Bluespotted Grouper Adrian Pingstone...24
Figure 33 Honeycomb Grouper Bernard DUPONT..24
Figure 34 Yellowtail Fusilier Nhobgood..25
Figure 35 Clownfish Nick Hobgood..25
Figure 36 Pink Anemonefish Bernd...25
Figure 37 Redbreasted Wrasse Jens Petersen..26
Figure 38 l Moon Wrasse Leonard Low..26
Figure 39 Bluestreak Cleaner Wrasse Divervincent..27
Figure 40 Butterflyfish Leonardo Stabile..27
Figure 41 Moray eel (*Gymnothorax thyrsoideus*) Bernard Dupont..28
Figure 42 Bannerfish fir0002..28
Figure 43 Titan Triggerfish Jan Derk..29
Figure 44 Ringed Angelfish...29
Figure 45 Sixstripe Angelfish Leonard Low..29
Figure 46 Damselfish..30
Figure 47 Parrotfish CC BY-SA 3.0, https://commons.wikimedia.org/w/index.php?curid=293543 ...30
Figure 48 Batfish Alain Feulvarch...30
Figure 49 Pufferfish *Sphoeroides spengleri* Andrew David..31
Figure 50 Goby and shrimp *Cryptocentrus cinctus* and *Alpheus bellulus* Nick Hobgood......31
Figure 51 Yellow-lipped Sea Krait...31

Index

Acanthaster planci, 18
Actinia, 13
Aeolides, 19
Amphiprion ocellaris, 25
Amphiprion perideraion, 25
anemones, 13
Angelfish, 29
Anthozoa, 13
Aristotle's Lantern, 18
Asteroidea, 18
bacterioplankton, 10
Balistoides viridescens, 29
Bannerfish, 28
Barracudas, 22
Batfish, 30
Blacktip Grouper, 24
Blacktip Reefshark, 22
Bluespotted grouper, 24
Bluespotted Ribbontail Ray, 21
Bluestreak Cleaner Wrasse, 27
Bony Fish, 22
Butterfly fish, 27
Camouflage, 11
Carangidae, 23
Carangoides fulvoguttatus, 23
Carcharhinus melanopterus, 22
Cartilaginous Fish, 21
Chaetodontidae, 27
Cheilinus fasciatus, 26
Chelonia, 19
Chelonia mydas, 20
Chevron Barracuda, 23
Chondrichthyes, 21
Christmas tree worm, 16
Clownfish, 25
Cnidaria, 13
Commensalism, 11
coral, 3, 13
Coral, 7, 14
coral reef, 14
Crown of Thorns, 18
Damselfish, 30
decomposers, 10
Dorids, 19
Echinoderms, 17
Echinoidea, 18
ecosystem, 9
Epinephelinae,, 24

Epinephelus fasciatus, 24
Epinephelus merra, 24
Eretmochelys imbricata, 20
fake eye, 12
food chain, 10
food network, 10
Giant Barracuda, 23
Giant Travelly, 23
Gobies, 31
Gobiidae, 31
Green Turtle, 20
Groupers, 24
Harlequin Grouper, 26
herbivore, 9
hermaphrodite, 8
Holothuroidea, 17
Honeycomb Grouper, 24
invertebrates, 12
jellyfish, 13
Jellyfish, 14
kleptocnidae, 19
Labroides dimidiatus, 27
larvae, 13
Laticauda colubrine, 31
medusa, 13
mimicry, 12
Moon Wrasse, 27
Moray Eel, 28
Muraenidae, 28
Mutualism, 11
mycoplankton, 10
natural selection, 8, 9, 11, 12
nekton, 10
niche, 7
Nudibranchia, 19
Nudibranchs, 19
omega-3 fatty acids, 10
Osteichthyes, 22
Parasitism, 11
Parrotfish, 30
parthogenesis, 8
phyto-plankton, 10
Pink Anemonefish, 25
Pistol Shrimp, 31
Plankton, 10
Platax teira, 30
Plectorhinchus chaetodonoides, 26

Pomacanthi,, 29
Pomacentri, 30
Porifera, 12
primary carnivores, 9
primary consumers, 9
primary producers, 9
protandreus, 8
protogyn, 8
Pufferfish, 31
Rabbitfish, 28
Redbreasted Wrasse, 26
regeneration, 18
Rhincodon typus, 21
Scaridae, 30
Scyphozoa, 13
Scyphozoans, 14
Sea anemones, 13
Sea cucumbers, 17
Sea Turtles, 19
Sea urchins, 18
secondary carnivores, 10
sequential hermaphrodite, 8
sexual reproduction, 8
sexual selection, 8
Siginidae, 28
Sphyraena, 22
Sphyraena barracuda, 23
Sphyraena flavicauda, 22
Sphyraena genie, 23
Spirobranchus giganteus, 16
Sponges, 12
Starfish, 18
symbiotic relationships, 11
Tenioura lymma, 21
Thalassoma lunare, 27
The Hawksbill Turtle, 20
Titan Triggerfish, 29
Trevally, 23
vertebrates, 12
Whale shark, 21
Yellow-lipped Sea Krait, 31
Yellowspotted travelly, 23
Yellowtail Barracuda, 22
Yellowtail Fusilier, 25
zoöplankton, 10
zooxanthellae, 13

Printed in Great Britain
by Amazon